Palewell Press

In the Alyscamps

Derek Summers

In the Alyscamps

Printed and bound in the United Kingdom
Published by Palewell Press http://palewellpress.co.uk

First Edition

ISBN 978-0-9556770-5-2

All Rights Reserved. Copyright ©2016 Derek Summers. No part of this publication may be reproduced or transmitted in any form or by any means, without permission in writing from the author.

Cover image is the painting *"Der Spaziergang"* by DiegoVoci™. Sincere thanks to *The Diego Voci™ Estate* for permission to use the image.

The photograph of Derek Summers on the back cover is Copyright © Richard Simmons, photographer 2016.

The collection's cover design is Copyright © Sheridan Reeve 2016

Dedication

To Carol who has walked with me in The Alyscamps in Arles and has been my supportive companion in the many avenues of life. I am particularly indebted to her for her care and support during my recent illness.

Acknowledgements

"Sherolyn deals with death" was published in The Interpreter's House, "Prière de Composter vos Billets" in The French Literary review, "In the Alyscamps" and "The Bleaching Gounds" in the Letterpress Poets Anthology.

My grateful thanks to friend and fellow poet George Beddow and to John Boaler, wise and astute reader and fellow enthusiast for 20th century poetry, for reading this selection and ensuring it was put together corrected and in a suitable order. My gratitude also to publisher Camilla Reeve for her efficiency and wise editing.

Contents

Prière de composter vos billets 7
Libération 8
Portbail en Fête 9
July 2014 10
In the Alyscamps Summer 2008 11
The Bleaching Grounds 12
'Inalienably and for all time' 13
Fire Falls in the Yosemite Valley 14
Oisans Midsummer 15
In Chichester Cathedral 17
In Leipzig and Dresden 18
Birdsong 20
Lepidoptera 21
The Young Fools 22
Reverse 24
Rat 25
The Lazy Jellyfish 26
Sherolyn deals with death 27
Stan Gammons Coaches 28
My Dutch Uncle 29
Scythian Warrior 30
Blake and the Volcano 31
Before the Feast/Ottoman Pottery 32
Marx and Heine in Paris 33

Two Russian Fragments 34

Tintin in Hornchurch 36

Keep taking the tabloids 37

Reconstructing Pleasure 38

All that stuff 39

Knots and Hitches 40

Not Hannibal Lecter 41

Amour 42

Love in an age of letters 43

My real rabbis 44

Death of a Poet 45

Loss 46

Derek Summers - Biography 47

Prière de composter vos billets

On my way to the graffiti-scratched Gents
on the platform at Valognes
I pass the ticket validation
machine with its strange invocation:
'Prière de composter vos billets'.

After the long trek to the shrine
their card was stamped.
Hence the name: Santiago 'de Compostela.'

Once in the South West
we followed the pilgrim route for a few kilometres
and found a bathing place in the chalk stream:
a rounded groove worn by countless backsides,
a graffiti scallop shell in the rock.

Paperwork, ablutions, a life, sorted.

Should I now walk to Finisterre,
to the end of the earth, to Compostela
to have my ticket stamped?

Libération

'Libération' is nuanced differently
for Monsieur Cuquemerle,
mayor and farmer
whose Norman farmhouse
was occupied by German officers
during the second World War.

He holds up our car
as he guides his cows
behind a barrier of well-used string.

Our patient incarceration
is rewarded with a smiling
'Je vais vous libérer maintenant'

Portbail en Fête

'Retreat with flaming torches'
at the end of the festivities?

Are these locals retreatniks,
creatures of our popular press,
inured to defeat by habit and history?
Are they like sad miners marching back
behind their colliery band?

No, I've heard the word elsewhere;
Monsieur Phollope: after school, farm, army, factory,
keeping the municipal campsite in military order,
finally took his 'retraite':

a life well-spent, exchanged for time
in an armchair.

So, after a day well spent
We'll stride home with flaming torches.

July 2014

*A Normandy village celebrates the day of its liberation in 1944;
war again in Gaza*

Who flew hawks and sparrows
above those trenches,
sowed willow herb in craters,
sent glistening creatures
amongst the mud and fractured iron?

Is the fire the spark
which broke at dusk
on swifts and swallows,
flared the barricades
crashed upon these beaches,
flashes now across our screens
from a land
once called holy?

They celebrate their moment
of liberation with *feux d'artifices.*

In the Alyscamps Summer 2008

You used to say 'We jog along well enough together'
I recall how we clasped hands desperately
at uncertain moments
as when the aircraft left the runway.

It seems to me that our hands touch more frequently now
on ordinary occasions:
in the taxi on the way to the hospital,
just crossing a road.

In the ancient cemetery road of the Alyscamps in Arles
we lean together:
the line of sarcophagi and cypresses leading inexorably forward.

On our long amble we are distracted for a while
by what we fancy to be nightingales.
Then, in the gloom of St Honorat's chapel,
are surprised to glimpse, through a round hole in the dome,
a dazzling disc of sky.

The Bleaching Grounds

They grow a dazzling whiteness
under the scant sun
of these northern towns.

Grey cloth laid out for months
becomes sheets, table linen, shrouds,
blank canvases to catch the eye.

Outside Haarlem, Jacob and Vincent
see them in fields that will later
hold crops, host burials.

Then Vincent awakes alone in Arles
to a blinding light
whose whiteness pulses

cobalt skies magenta poppies chrome yellow sun.
For a while he cannot see
that darkening figure crossing the field.

'Inalienably and for all time'

A letter records how Lincoln
snatched a moment from the war
to grant Yosemite to a free nation.

The indigenous Ahwaneechee
who owned no writing
could hear the sound of rhetoric

but feared that the great spirit
who cast those monster rocks
about the valley, might do so again

leaving no place to use or conserve
between the cliffs. For them it was
yoh-sem-it-ee: the place of killers.

Fire Falls in the Yosemite Valley

*'For nearly 100 years crowds would gather
in summer at the Curry Camp. . .'*

hot to see fire fall
three thousand feet,
ready to kill for a place.

A contrived meteor shower
might outblaze
that parched water path.

last minute jostling
inflamed
grasping at a wonder:

'Are you ready in the valley?'
'We are ready, Glacier Point!'
in thunderous affirmation:

a moment's sizzling anticipation

a torrent of red bark embers
hissing   over the cliff face

fuse of anticipation   ignited

quenched

Oisans Midsummer

Halfway to the highest pass
it is the still heart of summer

We loll exhausted beside the path
the green hillside peppered with flowers.

Across the valley, higher
than our eyes seem to tell

further than our hands
sense they could reach

The Meije Glacier
rolls its snout over the edge of the mountain

faces us like a cartoon nose
over a massive wall

and seems to ask
"Wot, no more climbing?"

We breathe the moment
in this far, high place

surrounded by colours
which recall forgotten meadows

and brave incongruities
of gardens in the suburb.

                      /continued

Oisans Midsummer - continued

Viewed through the telephoto
the glacier reveals

sharp cliffs of white
deep clefts of green-blue sea,

grey sweating ice feeding a reservoir
through rock-strewn wastes.

At night an immense
crystal solidity returns.

In the refuge, water arrives by
hosepipe, light by bottled gas or paraffin;

the chalet further up the valley
shows as a flickering light

like 'Evening Star'
Wordsworth's shepherd Michael's cottage,

but marks a holidaying
not a labouring occupant.

A high jet flashes. It appears silent
amongst the shooting stars.

In Chichester Cathedral

in Chichester Cathedral
I turned from Larkin's Arundel Tomb
sat down
and wept. What magnificent untruth.
the clasped hands
absurd little dogs
a general failure to read the poem:
'untruth',
a triple qualification
'our almost instinct, almost true'

Still touching our desperate need
for love,
endlessly altered though we are.

In Leipzig and Dresden

Thomaskirche

Your man
in blue jeans
begins the kyrie

Perhaps
you are
somewhere here

In the shadows
of those
paintings?

Behind
Bach's great
organ pipes

whose thunder
masks
my frail hopes?

Better perhaps
look sidewise
than up.

Frauenkirche

As the peace bell rings
a release of sunlight
flames the baroque gilded cross
proffered by a cloud of angels.

I look down
at words from Coventry

Vater vergib   (Coventry?)
Vater vergib   (Dresden?)
Vater vergib   (Hiroshima?)
Vater vergib   (Baghdad?)

Can repetition
or any amount
of blasting Bach
from an historic organ
bring forgiveness?

Birdsong

Early
the resident crows
croak their bleak

Later
on hedge, on peartree
on bay, on grass
a mild symphony of chirps, tweets
warbling, full-throated song

Some lesser crows toss themselves from the hedgerow
a scattering of black confetti

Suddenly
a hawk dips over the roof
a whirr of small wings
a gathering,
A roller motion escape over the crows' pine.

Mid afternoon
buzzards wheel
we hear their narrow cries

At dusk the crows
bleak their croak

Lepidoptera
after R.S. Thomas

You have made your god big
laying at his door
the great explosion
which you believe
brought about our universe.

I think of him rather
as a butterfly
bewildered in the autumn sunshine
grazing my cheek like a lover's eyelash
so that the hairs on my neck
stand on end; blundering

into a fellow creature
in dazed pursuit
of the unexpected lees of summer.
I have seen one resting
on a stone and recognized
a fellow wanderer whose

gawdy markings made me think
of a shared magnificence. I have
also seen one snatched from the air
by a small raptor or crushed
between the fingers
of someone like you or me.

The Young Fools
after Philip Larkin

What do they think will happen, the young fools,
To keep them like this? Do they somehow suppose
It's cool to wear low-rider jeans or have a boob job
And that they'll be the same in their wedding tent, on their world cruise
Or queuing blue-rinsed for a slot machine at Vegas?
Do they fancy that the bungee drop and skateboard swirl
Will last for ever? If so, will they ever
      Pause for thought about what comes after?

The ecstatic moment of drink or drugs, or movement
Shoulders aside the tedious thought of after and before
And hazards this intricate frail machine
Which sees, hears, chooses, acts
Yet finds itself reported Friday nights
Unconscious on the street or staggering
High-heeled with knickers round its feet.
      How can they do it?

Perhaps being young is to have a set of screens
Inside your head with landscapes flickering by:
People, shops, adventures, cosmic flights, perils
Flown over as on some magic virtual carpet,
Jet-propelled emitting lighted diodes. Do the screens
They see dissolve and reassemble
Into perpetual newness? They love what's new
      Which is why they look away

From shambling age, teetering
On the edge of a crevasse past which
These young fools glide like avatars
But not themselves. Should they fall in, they'll find
Another proxy new made-up, de-haired, tattooed and trimmed
To face the mall which masks the abyss
Where perhaps they'll game and shop for ever.
    Only time will tell.

Reverse
after Philip Larkin

They fuck you back your cherished kids
They really mean it, oh, they do.
driven by their wanton ids
they blame it all on you. And you!

But they'll be screwed up in their turn
by girls and boys in latest gear
who leave, only to return
succumbing with a pouting sneer.

We blame ours and they blame theirs.
They'd like to go but they can see
on grim, perpetual moving stairs
in life's new mall: KIDS GO FREE.

Rat
after George Macbeth

is my favourite. Who skitters
across rafters in the night,
rat-tracking. Is a scavenger
scuttling stores. Ran-
sacking food is

what he's at. See
him skulking near
graves and trash. Ah
would you bite rotting meat
if you might?

In Room 101 rat
and his mates tear
at your face. In famine
rat comes like the plague. Rat
lives by the teeth of his gut.

Antenna-whiskers, dragging tail.
Scattered litter. A rent
in the sack. The
grain rack empty. Am
a rat. Am a rat. Am a rat.

The Lazy Jellyfish

The lazy jellyfish
shockingly lacks sense;
content to float alone,
transparently amorphous,
worrying timid swimmers.

The leaping porpoise
is sociable,
has fun,
perhaps it has a purpose.

Sherolyn deals with death

Sherolyn accounts for death's estates
whisked by satellite-guided Audi
to flagging family parlours and
weed-wrecked graveyards
releasing equity, providing
a consolidated service, slick as Microsoft,
clean as a MacDonald's bathroom
which today's bereaved
have every right to expect.

She finds the work invigorating
her clients caring people, the firm, Christian.
Does what she can
to make the best of this part of our lives
rarely forgetting that despite all she controls
she is not immune

her rash of freckles growing in the sun.

Stan Gammons Coaches

It was usually Stan who coached us
his quote invariably the lowest –
risk-assessment was not in the price.

He would arrive just a few minutes late
with an unfailing sense
of when the tardiest student
would have arrived.
His bus looked more 1950's than 70's:
tartan moquette, chromed rails
and he in tweed turn-ups
hoist high above his rounded belly, check shirt,
leather belt, braces, a cable knit sleeveless slipover,
puffing at a pipe as he drove
tantalisingly slowly
but always getting you there in time
as if the roundabouts and lights were phased
to his personal rhythm.

On one rare occasion, Stan, agreed to make use of a spare ticket.
It was Pinter's Caretaker.
What did he think?
'Dunno what the owd boy was on about.
It were bloody funny!
Next time I'll have a kip on the bus.'

My Dutch Uncle

sits at the window
of his Saxon farmhouse

puffs at the fragrant mixture
in his meerschaum

admires the windpump
at the side of the polder

eyes a print
of an immaculate interior

fingers receipts for payments of tax
local, regional, national

senses the warmth
from the pot-bellied stove

would be astounded
to feel his clogs

detach and batter his ankles
caught in the swirl of the North Sea

Scythian Warrior

This is one of several poems inspired by exhibits at the Ashmolean Museum, Oxford, in this case, a painted and damaged cast of an ancient statue.

So you lost
your head, torso and
part of your leg
but kept your trousers
painstakingly restored
to vivid harlequin patchwork.

You are no longer what you were:
classicist's chaste lust,
excuse for centuries
of naked beauty.

You ride in fun-fair gaudy,
legs rivalling
the folksy decoration
of the narrowboats
on our canal.

Blake and the Volcano

For the exhibition: William Blake Apprentice and Master

Volcanogod

sparked us out

ash

Blake

felt the effulgence

        dreamed

tyger   lamb

settling

each side

of the fell

Before the Feast

Inspired by Ottoman Pottery gallery

Could sizzling lemon-doused
fillets outswim
a blue promise waiting
in its sleek glazed pond?

Might aromatic sweetness
outbid
the seductive enameled sharpness
of these glistering grapes

juice-oozing roasted pheasants
outfly these
winging by woods
for ever in a crystal air?

already there
before the feast was served

fish   flesh   fowl
flowers   leaves

bright
living
sharp

Marx and Heine in Paris

Poet Heinrich and his young cousin Karl
get rat-arsed in Paris
on absinthe in the Faubourg
on socialism in the Café de la Régence
on philosophy at the Bibliotèque Nationale

Karl supplies the absinthe
Heinrich, at rare lucid moments, metaphors

'What have the workers to lose?'
Heine borrows manacles from Blake
adds that religion keeps them going
as he in his ill-health is sustained by laudanum

Karl guzzles the poet's words.
Parched in the dusty arena of
the library he burps back

Religion is the opium of the masses
They have nothing to lose but their chains

Two Russian Fragments

Written after visiting Perm and St Petersburg, September 2010

1

Catch the tram along Petropavola.
Note the unsmiling conductress.
Return by Lenin Street,
glimpse the imperious driver.

Window-shop at Ecco or Hugo Boss
or choose from a thousand items
in the street kiosk.
Fix your eyes on your choice:
a small window will open.
Pass through your roubles.

Visit the public library
where Zhivago met Lara or
stroll down the Konsomol Prospekt
to the Kama River and take tea
on a river cruiser, long out of service.

Totter on high heels
across the tramlines and broken roadway
to the university:
'Read 'Vivat Academia, vivant professores' on the wall.
Ask questions, speak your mind

though Gulag 36 still stands
lost amongst the birches
under a dazzling sky
which your professors saw only at night
through a square metre of barbed wire.

2

Visit the opera house:
its classical façade
still bears its hammer and sickle.

Here ballerinas danced
before tsars, before Lenin and Stalin,
Kruschev and Putin.

Learn at the museum of Soviet History
not far from the palace in Petrograd
where Matisse's 'Dancers' was commissioned

how Lenin made his office
in this house of a dancer
and laid his revolver across her desk.

Tintin in Hornchurch

That sparkling shopwindow reflection shows not my cornfield quiff but Douglas Hurd, backview, apparently not waiting to replace a prime minister with Y Fronts over his pinstripe pants – 'They also stand who only sit and wait.' Music drifts across the high street; Mario Lanza is Caruso or The Student Prince in love for the first time with an heraldic bierstein whose polished tapa reflects a yellow and chestnut Marmite jar. It's showing at the Essoldo. Has my animator forgotten waffles or at least Frîtes med Mayonnase? The Christmas lights supplier at least is doing well. Am I sculpted in neon to fight off Captain Haddock's enemies from Romford or flying with the few over distant Hyde Park as the raiders spiral down in a coil of illuminated smoke? On Cosmic Boulevard a robin-breasted inflatable Santa flashes: off – on, off – on; croaks Me...rry...Chr...ist...mas...Ha...ppy...New...Year. What does Snowy know?

Keep taking the tabloids

Look at the tabloids
They're polychrome and full of tits

Read the tabloids
They're full of itzy tasty bits

Keep reading the tabloids
They're hot on sport and short on news

You'll love tabloid opinion
Slickly designed to reflect your views

Keep buying the tabloids
They love celebs but give them hell

Buy the tabloids
They're black and white but only figuratively

Keep taking the tabloids
Not the broadsheets

Keep taking the tabloids
You're not a bearded liberal twit

Reconstructing Pleasure

Scattered on a woodland track:
tyre marks (recent)
one cigarette packet (empty)
two plastic sandwich packs (void)
one cigarette card (discarded)
one crumpled condom (used)
four cigarette butts (half-smoked)

Can we construct a narrative?

Snatched impromptu lunchbreak:
tyres, cigarette, sandwich, cigarette, condom, tyres

Routine encounter:
tyres, condom, cigarette, sandwich, cigarette, tyres

Cheating on partner or firm?
Pure romance?

With this frail evidence
who can tell? But
given today's forensics
people might be less careless
with their litter.

All that stuff

Don't pay too much for all that stuff.
Read this, I'll give you some for free.
Don't let it weigh you down, be tough,
sort it, send it to the dump; you'll see
it's only matter and it doesn't.
Don't give a toss for what you chuck away:
it was and now it isn't
though still there in a funny sort of way.

But some things seem designed to last:
ideas, hopes, promises,
stuff dug up from the past
not lost, you hope; but made to clutch
against time's demolition

Knots and Hitches
- a badge for cub scouts

The badge came as no surprise
I could still feel the midwife's tug
at my navel, the surgeon at my abdomen

my mother's hand showing without words
how to cast on and the meticulous line of knots
which became that little blue

bib and brace swimming suit in which
I viewed trawlermen at rest from the perils
of which we sang, mending nets

to be cast to catch our fish suppers
at the harbour café. Later the gauze
touch of a chiffon scarf to cover my nakedness

after I tumbled into the lake in the park.
I had not yet read of the hangman who
might make his good noose at my nape

or the net of agreements and contracts
tightly drawn, to be tied and untied
in my life's ragged fustian

And I wonder
will the knitters be there
at the text's scaffold?

Not Hannibal Lecter

They clip me to the gurney by my mask.
I don't bite. I don't squirm.
The X-Rays might sear me at the wrong spot.
The warning signal, then the whirring and creaking.

I attempt to make the time pass
inwardly reciting favorite poems.

At a certain point the rays spark my optic nerve:

'and the fire that breaks from thee then'. . .

Amour

For a tottering moment
they are the lovers that they were.

He must manoeuvre her from wheelchair
to armchair. For a fraction they face each other
in the old way. He rounds her in his arms,
eases from the stool, pulls up her pants.

She spits water in his face, he slaps back
but hands will sometimes reach,
find fragments of their song

Love in an age of letters
for Tania

Love, live on parting lips
could not linger even eight long days
before his letters came:

they were too full of daily stuff –
'he'd studied hard, his sister came,
his mother'd baked a cake.'

The week was all too full of days.
She tried the public phone but
love played hide and seek

around the impatient Russian operator's
coughs and sighs and bleeps.
Hard too to read his love amongst the netiquette

of Facebook, Messenger or Twitter.
Seven score characters
still held space for doubts.

Then Luvtext™ came: ten letters,
just room enough to spell
'♡ he loves me/loves me not.'

My real rabbis
for Jim Harrop

are these hills
and those who
have crossed before.

I seek their memorials
on the misty tops
their markers amongst the maze of peat.

Leaving
I place a stone
to mark our passing.

Death of a Poet

The snug pen
tumbles from your hand
your book fallen shut

vowel-road
closed

rhyme-trek
barred

word-horde
silenced

image-store
snapped tight

The peat-born road shudders
as you are carried back
across that strife-
frayed border.

Loss

I felt I'd lost you when you went to work
but found my own way home.
When we first lost you to the hospital
a neighbour found us; losing our fingers in snapdragons.
She's lost now among the roses below her verandah.

For years I lost you in my own life
but found you yearly, scratched and stung by blackberries.
Later you'd lose yourself picking our cherries,
emerging dazed and spattered,
taken, at last by morphine, then by fire.

Scattering your ashes on water, I find you again
somehow in brambles and cherry blossom.

Derek Summers - Biography

Derek was brought up and educated in North West London. He studied English Literature, French and Philosophy and taught poetry to non-traditional students including craft apprentices and returners to study, in Nottingham, Bedford and Luton.

Derek believes poetry provides redress to some of life's wounding experiences and that it can speak truth about power, if not to it. He is the editor of an anthology produced with old Labour politician Michael Foot: *The Foots and the Poets, Poetry and a Political Family* (Jarndyce, 2010).

Derek's work has been published in *The Interpreter's House*, *French Literary Review*, in *brevities: 20 short poems* (2012). He was highly commended in the 2014 Sentinel International Poetry Competition and has contributed recently to the Oxford Ashmolean Museum's Ekphrasis Poetry project.

Palewell Press

Palewell Press is a small independent publisher handling poetry, fiction and non-fiction with a particular interest in human rights, social history and the environment. Writers on these subjects who are looking for publication should, in the first instance, send ten pages of their work to enquiries@palewellpress.co.uk

www.ingramcontent.com/pod-product-compliance
Lightning Source LLC
LaVergne TN
LVHW041551060526
838200LV00037B/1238